CoolBrands® 2011/12 An insight into some of Britain's coolest brands

2011/12
CoolBrands.uk.com

05

Chief Executive
Ben Hudson

Managing Editor
Laura Hill

Brand Liaison Director
Liz Silvester

Brand Liaison Manager
Heidi Smith

Head of Accounts
Will Carnochan

Publishing Agency
August Media
augustmedia.com

For August Media
Editor-In-Chief
Kitty Finstad
Art Director
Ian Taylor
Senior Designer
Adele Carpenter
Chief Sub Editor
Kate Lloyd
Production Manager
Mário da Silva

Published by
Superbrands (UK) Ltd
22-23 Little Portland Street
London
W1W 8BU

Colour reproduction by
Wyndeham Pre-Press

Printed in Italy

ISBN: 978-0-9565334-2-5

All rights reserved.

© 2011 Superbrands (UK) Ltd
CoolBrands® is a registered trademark of Superbrands (UK) Ltd
in the United Kingdom.

MIX
Paper from
responsible sources
FSC® C015829

Foreword

07

As CoolBrands® celebrates its 10th year, Rob da Bank reflects on what cool means to him...

'It dawns on me that it's often the simplest ideas that make a cool product, brand or company. As someone who spends an unhealthy amount of time with headphones jammed in my ears, the music world has become simpler with the advent of the MP3, and it can be argued that reading has become easier, and more lightweight, with the arrival of the e-book – two simple but revolutionary ideas in media.

As a slight technophobe, who still plays good old-fashioned vinyl at many of my gigs, I don't queue up for the latest i-whatever, yet somehow my house is full of must-have stuff. There's my iPad and BlackBerry blinking away on the kitchen table as the computer updates Twitter and Facebook, the Blu-ray shows cartoons while Sky+ records the cricket, and the Wi-Fi box keeps it all ticking over.

But it's just as much the more left-field things that make me happy – kids' shoes with in-built wheels, sleeping bags with arms and legs attached, dry shampoo, the world's smallest car, The Wire and Oyster cards. Indeed, where would we be without Angry Birds? So as we embrace another decade in our Brave New World, I'm still not sure I know what cool is, but I'm sure you'll find out in this very book.'

Rob da Bank
Founder & curator of Bestival, owner of Sunday Best Recordings, Radio 1 DJ, ambassador of the Independent Music Chart, and CoolBrands® Expert Council member

Contents

09

About
CoolBrands®

11

CoolBrands® is an annual initiative to identify and pay tribute to the nation's coolest brands. Since 2001 we have been canvassing the opinions of experts and consumers to produce an annual barometer of Britain's coolest brands, people and places.

In addition to this book, the 2011/12 CoolBrands® are celebrated online at CoolBrands.uk.com and in print via our national media supplement. Each brand featured in this, the 10th annual programme, has qualified for inclusion based on the collective opinions of the independent and voluntary Expert Council and more than 2,000 members of the British public. Further details of the selection process are provided overleaf.

The annual CoolBrands® programme is administered by Superbrands (UK) Ltd. Superbrands was launched in London in 1995 and is now a global business operating in more than 55 countries worldwide.

What is a CoolBrand?

Cool is subjective and personal. Accordingly, voters are not given a definition but are asked to bear in mind the following factors, which research has shown are inherent in all CoolBrands®...

13

Style
Innovation
Originality
Authenticity
Desirability
Uniqueness

Brands do not apply or pay to be considered for CoolBrands® status.

Who chooses the CoolBrands®?

The 2011/12 CoolBrands® were chosen by an Expert Council and thousands of members of the British public. The entire selection process is independently administered by The Centre for Brand Analysis – visit CoolBrands.uk.com for full details.

15

The 2011/12 Expert Council

Walé Adeyemi MBE	Fashion Designer
Kate Creasey	Former Editor, Cosmopolitan.co.uk
Rob da Bank	DJ & Bestival Founder
Ben de Lisi	Fashion Designer
James-lee Duffy	Art Director, Graphic Designer & Illustrator, We Are Shadows
Gizzi Erskine	TV Chef
Sadie Frost	Actress & Fashion Designer
Kate Halfpenny	Fashion Designer & Stylist
Ruby Hammer MBE & Millie Kendall MBE	Founders, Ruby & Millie
Newby Hands	Associate Editor & Director of Health & Beauty, Harper's Bazaar
Rickie Haywood-Williams & Melvin Odoom	Hosts, Kiss Breakfast Show
Kelly Hoppen MBE	Designer
Jessie J	Music Artist
Jo Jackson	Managing Director, 'i-am' beyond
Dolly Jones	Editor, VOGUE.COM
Daisy Knights	Jewellery Designer
Mark Krendel	Partnerships Director, Universal Music Group UK
Lee Lapthorne	Fashion & Creative Director
Hannah Marshall	Designer
Zara Martin	TV Presenter & Model
Liz Matthews	Entertainment Publicist
Kay McMahon	Digital Director, Wallpaper*
Natasha McNamara	Editor, GLAMOUR.com
James Murphy	Founding Partner, adam&eve
Miquita Oliver	Broadcaster
Steve Parkinson	Managing Director, Kiss
Paul Percival & Adam Reed	Managing Director / Creative Director, Percy & Reed
Way Perry	Fashion Director, Man About Town
Danny Sangra	Artist, Art Director & Designer
Stuart Semple	Artist
Lisa Snowdon	Presenter, Model & Co-Host, Capital Breakfast Show
Tim Soar	Menswear & Womenswear Designer
Anna-Marie Solowij	Beauty Journalist & Brand Consultant
Nadja Swarovski	VP International Communications & Creative Director, Swarovski
Jo Tutchener	Founder, Beauty Seen PR
Grace Woodward	TV Presenter & Stylist
Stephen Cheliotis	Chief Executive, The Centre for Brand Analysis & Chairman, CoolBrands® Expert Council

Turn to page 150 for more about the Expert Council

The
Brands

17

Abel & Cole

Abel & Cole started out with a grin and a bag of spuds in 1988 and is now synonymous with seasonal and healthy, home-delivered organic food.

Abel & Cole proves you don't have to knit your own yogurt to eat healthy, ethically sourced food. It has delivered high-quality food from small, independent food makers to switched-on households since 1988, developing close, trusting relationships with farmers and producers. It helps customers enjoy and understand sustainable, seasonal eating. It minimises food waste and unnecessary packaging – using boxes, not bags, since day one – and promotes biodiversity and animal welfare alongside fair trade and organic farming.

abelandcole.co.uk

Affordable Art Fair

The Affordable Art Fair is the leading showcase for contemporary art under £4,000. Its formula is simple, yet unique: a relaxed, inspiring environment and a diverse range of quality contemporary art.

Launched in London in 1999, the Affordable Art Fair (AAF) has revolutionised the art market with its fun and accessible approach, and is now a stand-out fixture in the UK arts calendar. More than 100 galleries offer a huge array of art with pieces by established names sitting alongside work by the emerging stars of tomorrow. AAF has become a global phenomenon with fairs taking place across Europe, Australia, America and Asia.

affordableartfair.com

Apple

Sleek, stylish design combined with powerful, groundbreaking technology make Apple's unique products iconic must-haves around the world.

Apple ignited the personal computer revolution in the 1970s with Apple II and reinvented the personal computer in the 1980s with the Macintosh. Today, Apple continues to lead the industry in innovation with its award-winning computers and has spearheaded the digital media revolution with the iPod and iTunes online store. Furthermore, Apple reinvented the mobile phone with its revolutionary iPhone and App Store, and in March 2011 launched the iPad 2, which is set to define the future of mobile media and computing devices.

apple.com

Asahi

Sophisticated, pure and refreshing, Asahi Super Dry is the number one beer in Japan and the leading super premium beer in the UK.

With its clean, crisp taste, Asahi Super Dry is the premium beer of choice at top bars, restaurants and clubs across the UK. The brand prides itself on innovation, building the world's first robotic barman and recently unveiling the Asahi Toyota FJ Cruiser – a 4x4 that serves draught beer from its boot. Asahi sponsors the best events across the UK and has its own bar within the grandeur of London's Royal Albert Hall.

asahibeer.co.uk

Aspall Cyder

The recipes for Aspall's unique blend of bittersweet and culinary apples have been handed down through eight generations of the Chevallier family since 1728.

The Aspall philosophy is quality without compromise, focusing on producing the very best range of super-premium cyders. Apples are graded by eye and to this day the Chevallier family insists on signing off every batch, ensuring quality remains first and foremost. As a result, the premium quality of the cyder is consistently recognised with a multitude of awards including the coveted prize of World's Best Cider for two consecutive years.

aspall.co.uk

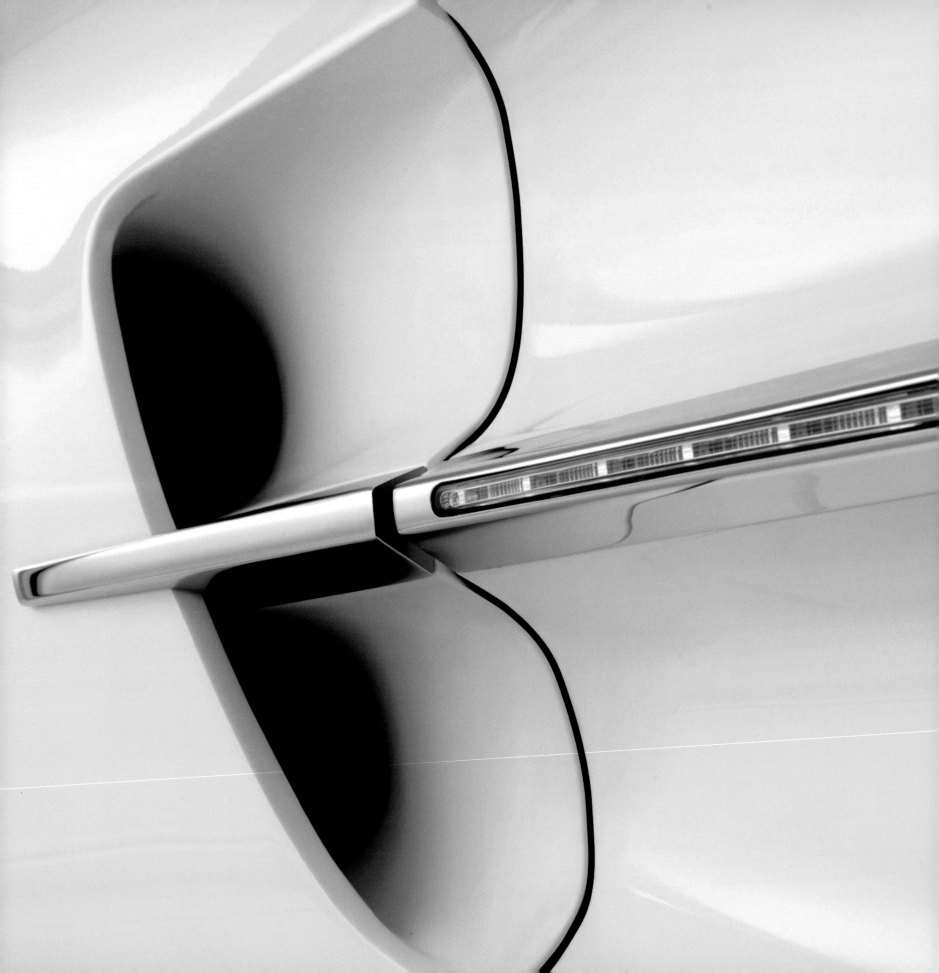

Aston Martin

Elegant design, perfect proportions, hand-finished luxury and impeccable attention to detail: every Aston Martin brings power and sporting ability together with true refinement and understated beauty.

An Aston Martin has a distinctive and individual character, honed over decades of highly skilled design and manufacturing. Founded in 1913, it has produced some of the world's most celebrated and iconic sports cars – pure driving machines that combine bold, elegant forms with exceptional ability. In 2011, Aston Martin's new models – from the tailor-fit Cygnet city car to the limited-edition V12 Zagato, and ultra rare One-77 – demonstrate the brand's skill, agility and desire for innovation.

astonmartin.com

Aveda

Rooted in more than 30 years of environmental and social responsibility, Aveda is a premium botanical haircare and skincare brand that crafts professional, high-performance products.

The first beauty company to manufacture with 100 per cent wind power, Aveda has repeatedly set benchmarks for organic ingredient purchasing, naturally derived ingredients, environmental packaging, and partnerships with indigenous communities worldwide. Its annual Earth Month campaign unites its global network and has raised over $18 million for environmental causes to date. Aveda is also found backstage at New York Fashion Week, spreading its unique green style while living its mission: 'Beauty is as beauty does.'

facebook.com/aveda

BALTIC Centre for Contemporary Art

BALTIC's strong and playful brand mirrors the iconic building in which it is housed. Quality, integrity and accessibility are its brand values, while its personality is sophisticated, stylish and self-deprecating.

Housed in a landmark industrial building on the south bank of the River Tyne in Gateshead, BALTIC presents a dynamic, diverse and international programme of contemporary visual art. BALTIC has no permanent collection, providing instead an ever-changing calendar of innovative exhibitions and events that give a unique insight into contemporary artistic practice. 2011 sees BALTIC host the Turner Prize 2011, the first time it has been shown outside of a Tate venue.

balticmill.com

BALTIC

Bang & Olufsen

Distinctive design, unrivalled attention to detail and outstanding performance have helped Bang & Olufsen to become the world's leading luxury audio-visual and integrated solutions provider.

More than 86 years on, Bang & Olufsen remains true to the spirit of its founders: 'A never-failing will to create only the best,' as Peter Bang described it. That pursuit of perfection has created some of the audio-visual industry's most iconic products. Bang & Olufsen's design remains as individual as ever, matched by levels of innovation, quality and performance that consistently set new benchmarks.

bang-olufsen.com

BANG & OLUFSEN

BoConcept

BoConcept creates customised, coordinated and affordable design furniture for urban-minded individuals, while its expert advice for any interior design challenge is offered as standard.

Since 1952, BoConcept has been inspired by urban life across the globe to create functional, contemporary furniture that works within limited spaces. It's a design blueprint that goes hand-in-hand with customising furniture to fit individual needs. With the help of its in-store consultants and interior designers, BoConcept provides solutions that will fulfil a room's potential – and the customer's vision. For BoConcept, being urban-minded means modernity, energy and a passion for design and trends.

boconcept.co.uk

bulthaup

Characterised by architecture, precision and innovation, bulthaup creates kitchen spaces that expertly combine individuality and function with the understated beauty of exceptional materials.

From its origins in the foothills of the Alps in 1949 Germany, bulthaup has built a worldwide reputation for expertly crafted living spaces. Through technical perfection it creates kitchens that integrate seamlessly with the architecture of their surroundings, marrying function and form – never compromising on either. From pioneering intelligent installation concepts and the revolutionary workbench, to its philosophy to evolve alongside its customers, adapting to their individual needs, bulthaup delivers a truly unmistakeable service.

bulthaup.com

bulthaup

Champagne Perrier-Jouët

Since 1811, the House of Perrier-Jouët has been renowned for its boutique champagnes, which combine exceptional elegance with Belle Epoque *art de vivre*.

The avant-garde spirit for which Champagne Perrier-Jouët is fêted is embodied in the iconic Anemone bottle of its prestige cuvée, Belle Epoque, designed in 1902 by Art Nouveau master Emile Gallé. Perrier-Jouët celebrates its bicentenary with the launch of its 'Living Legacy' Cuvée Bi-Centenaire. Two magnums of Belle Epoque 1998 are encased in a diptych, sculpted by artist Daniel Arsham, one half of which can be stored for up to 100 years in a private section of the Perrier-Jouët cellars in Epernay, France.

perrier-jouet.com

Cinnamon Kitchen

Cinnamon Kitchen is a contemporary addition to the London restaurant scene, with award-winning interior design and a vibrant menu that showcases the very best in modern Indian cuisine.

Fittingly set in London's historic East India Company spice warehouse, Cinnamon Kitchen serves modern Indian cuisine inspired by the same ethos as its acclaimed sister restaurant, The Cinnamon Club, but in a more relaxed setting. Home to the capital's first tandoor bar and grill, Cinnamon Kitchen sees executive chef Vivek Singh and his team pushing culinary boundaries through their imaginative approach. The restaurant is complemented by its sleek bar, Anise, serving spice-infused cocktails in an intimate contemporary space.

cinnamon-kitchen.com

CINNAMON
Kitchen

Cirque du Soleil

Cirque du Soleil touches audiences' hearts and imaginations through emotion. Every show is an explosive sensory event that champions togetherness, acceptance, physical strength and beauty.

A creatively driven brand, Cirque du Soleil places live shows at its heart – 31 since its inception in 1984, seen by more than 100 million people worldwide. Each production has a unique concept and features handmade costumes, original music and state-of-the-art lighting. The Montréal-based company was founded by Guy Laliberté and a small band of itinerant street performers: accordionists, stilt walkers and fire-eaters. Today, it has 5,000 employees worldwide, including more than 1,300 performing artists.

cirquedusoleil.com

Cirque du Soleil and Sun Logo are owned by Cirque du Soleil and used under license. Images: Dominique Lemieux©2011 Cirque du Soleil, Jan Swikels©1999 Cirque du Soleil, Kym Barrett©2010 Cirque du Soleil, Renée April©2009 Cirque du Soleil

Cobra

Cobra is the refreshingly smooth premium beer inspired by today's India. It's brewed to an authentic Indian recipe, and given a modern twist to taste extra smooth.

Millennia of civilisation and a melting pot of cultures have created one of the most extraordinary places on earth – India. Today, India stands proudly on her roots but marches boldly into the 21st century in new, original ways. It is this progressive fusion of past and present that inspired Cobra, a modern twist adding extra smoothness to an authentic Indian recipe.

cobrabeer.com

Dave

Satirical and edgy, Dave is the home of witty banter and features the best in contemporary entertainment including QI, Mock the Week and Top Gear.

A well-established portal to a plethora of entertaining programming, Dave branched out in 2011 and is now creating its very own witty banter. The 'Made by Dave' shows include Dave's One Night Stand – featuring comedians such as Chris Addison and Greg Davies – Al Murray's Compete for the Meat pub quiz and Alexander Armstrong's own panel show. Off-screen, Dave's Comedy Society: Live sees the brand extend into live events, immersing its audience in its addictively irreverent humour.

joindave.co.uk

Dave

200th ISSUE

DAZED & CONFUSED

ACCELERATE!

GUEST-EDITOR

BJÖRK

SHOWS YOU THE FUTURE

WITH THE MOST MIND-EXPANDING SCIENTISTS,
ARTISTS AND TECH GEEKS IN THE WORLD

VOL.II I.100 AUGUST 2011
UK£3.95 US$5.99 MADE IN THE UK
IR£3.95 US $8.99 ¥1495 €5.94 ₱145

Dazed & Confused

Dazed & Confused magazine is an unparalleled trailblazer for emerging talent that aims to set the cultural agenda, both on and offline.

Founded by Jefferson Hack and Rankin in 1992, independent publication Dazed & Confused celebrates its 20th anniversary in 2012. The explosive British fashion, culture and arts magazine and its online component DazedDigital.com have a strong global reputation for editorial that is groundbreaking and supports each new generation of fashion, art, literature, photography and music talent. 2011 witnessed the arrival of Dazed Live – a major new creative festival for London featuring music, art, screenings and talks.

dazeddigital.com

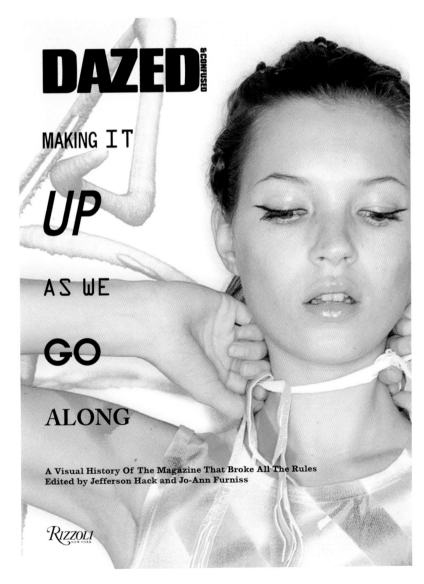

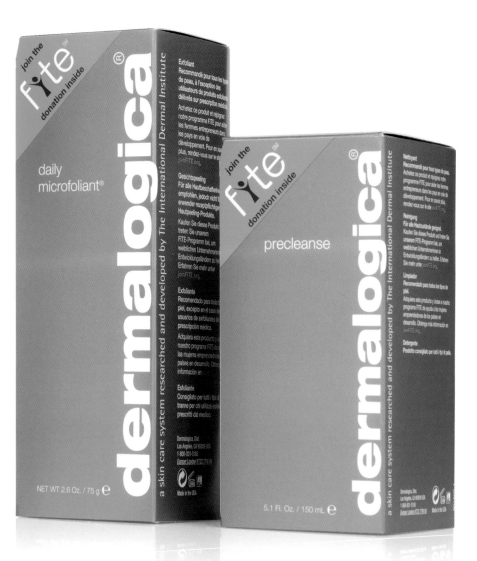

Dermalogica

Favoured by skincare professionals, Dermalogica is known for its simplicity of style and emphasis on skin health education – a unique approach that is both pure and progressive.

Promoting a no-nonsense approach to skincare since it was founded in the 1980s, Dermalogica resolutely avoids the irritants found in many beauty products. Its skincare system combines the best of science and nature, while professional consultation ensures consumers are confident in caring for their skin. Through the FITE initiative, the brand is now helping to empower people in a very different way, working to provide small business loans to women entrepreneurs in the developing world.

dermalogica.com

dermalogica®
a skin care system researched and developed by The International Dermal Institute

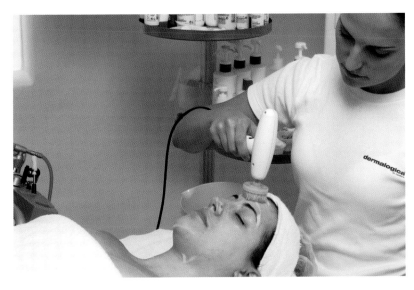

Ducati

A premium brand, Ducati conceives and produces sports motorcycles with exclusive Italian design, distinctive features and superior performance. Proven on racetracks all over the world.

Ducati's race-inspired motorcycles are characterised by unique engine features, innovative design and advanced engineering. Founded in 1926 in Bologna, Italy, Ducati has since created motorcycles across six model types, from Superbikes through to the groundbreaking new Diavel, which are sold in more than 80 countries worldwide. Competing in MotoGP since 2003, Ducati won the World Championship in 2007, and in World Superbikes has won more titles than all other motorcycle manufacturers combined.

ducatiuk.com

What is the **first direct** Lab?

The **first direct** Lab is all about getting you involved. It's a place where you can view new ideas and test-drive brand new **first direct** innovations before we release them, so you can tell us exactly what you think and have your say right from the start. After all, who better to test new ideas than the people they're aimed at... you?

SHARE

live tests ›

Live **tests**

Latest

first direct **QR codes**

Do you see QR codes as useful and innovative? Do you think they would be relevant to future pieces of **first direct** communication?

★★★☆☆ (24 ratings)

👤 **14 people** have commented on this

read more ›

Quick **question**
Tell us what you think!

Do you spend too much of your spare time getting life's everyday tasks done?

| Yes | ○ |
| No | ○ |

We ♥ve
This month we're loving

Pizza Express iPhone® app

Love it ♥   Hate it 💔

This month we're loving the Pizza Express iPhone app - it's handy, easy to use and available to download from iTunes now.

firstdirect.com **redesign concepts**

We're currently redesigning our website, and we'd love to hear your feedback on two potential homepages we've created: one tailored specifically for existing **first direct** customers, and one that's been designed with non-customers in mind.

★★★★☆ (130 ratings)

👤 **10 people** have commented on this

read more ›

Make a **suggestion**

Do you have a great idea? Tell us what you think should be in the Lab.

make a suggestion ›

Submit your **feedback**
We're here to listen

If you've had a look at any of our ideas and innovations then please tell us what you think of them. Just select the item, and click on 'leave your feedback'. This will take you to the feedback page.

Please select a Lab item to leave feedback on: | Click to select ▲▼ |

leave your feedback ›

first direct **Lab**

first direct Lab is a site that we've created to get people involved with our projects while they are still in development, so we can listen to your feedback and create the best solution possible. We'd like to start with the **first direct** Lab itself.

★★★★☆ (19 ratings)

👤 **13 people** have commented on this

read more ›

view all current Lab items ›

This is not **first direct's** primary website. All content featured are Beta versions. For accurate and reliable information, please visit **www.firstdirect.com** Android™ is a trademark of Google Inc. iPhone® is a trade mark of Apple Inc.

first direct

Apart from expert banking, talking with customers is what first direct does best, 24/7/365. Recent initiatives are encouraging customers to join the conversation.

first direct's people are recruited for their chat, not their banking experience – as 2011's 'Chatterbox' TV ad demonstrates. The spoof 'Buddy' viral underlined the bank's passion for customer service, while first direct Lab subscribes to the ethos of co-creation, using customer suggestions to develop new services. 2011 saw first direct launch its Facebook page and the UK's first transactional banking iPhone app. It was also named Which? Magazine's Best Financial Services Provider for the second year running.

firstdirect.com

first direct

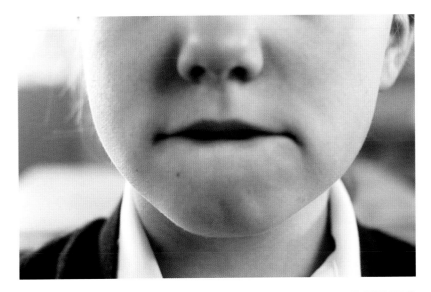

ghd

Celebrated and iconic, ghd has shaped the way women style their hair during the past decade in its own confident, glamorous and fashion-forward way.

Ten years after revolutionising hairstyling, ghd remains true to its founding ethos: the spirit of transformation. Its recently launched ghd Style range of styling products, and collection of professional brushes, complement the stylers, while brand ambassador Katy Perry epitomises ghd's essence of empowerment. With its Iconic Eras brand campaign shot by acclaimed photographer David LaChapelle, and a creative team bolstered by top stylists Zoe Irwin and Kenna, ghd is at the cutting edge of style.

ghdhair.com

Graham & Brown

Have you noticed the resurgence of wallpaper? Graham & Brown is responsible. With its innovative, imaginative and enviable heritage, it's a brand that constantly surprises with everything for the wall.

Celebrating its 65th anniversary in 2011, Graham & Brown has been doing things differently since 1946. Acknowledged for leading the revival of wallpaper through its innovative and desirable designs, it works with many renowned designers, from Barbara Hulanicki to Marcel Wanders, and also runs philanthropic projects with emerging designers and artists. The brand extends beyond wallpaper with coordinating wall art and its paint range, The Colours That Made Britain Great.

grahambrown.com

GRAHAM & BROWN

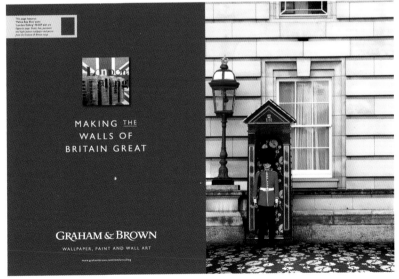

Green & Black's

British brand Green & Black's has been ethically trading cocoa, and making organic and Fair Trade chocolate, for nearly 21 years.

Green & Black's was built upon a pioneering ethos, embodying modern sustainability with its combination of exceptional taste and ethical codes of conduct. The brand came into being when founders Craig Sams and his wife Josephine Fairley discovered a unique-tasting cocoa bean in Belize, and the entrepreneurial spirit that defined the company's early years resonates to this day.

greenandblacks.com

H&M

With a philosophy that fashion and quality needn't come with a hefty price tag, H&M is synonymous with fun, affordable, trend-led clothing.

A high-street staple, H&M encourages people to find their own style. Created by in-house designers, its collections mix the latest trends with classic tailoring and essential basics – all at an accessible price and manufactured according to H&M's strict code of ethics. Collaborations with the likes of Versace, Stella McCartney and Jimmy Choo have received global recognition, while the brand's design nous has also been applied to the home, creating a range of fashionable textiles.

hm.com

Images: Andreas Sjödin, Johan Sandberg

Haunch of Venison

A contemporary art gallery based in London and New York, Haunch of Venison represents and exhibits some of the world's leading artists.

Founded in 2002, Haunch of Venison has emerged as one of the most dynamic commercial galleries in London's growing contemporary arts scene. Working with an international group of artists and designers, the gallery showcases both emerging and established talent. 2011 saw the gallery return to its original home in Haunch of Venison Yard, Mayfair, a historic 18th-century townhouse brilliantly reconfigured by leading architect Annabelle Selldorf as a 21st-century art gallery.

haunchofvenison.com

HAUNCH OF VENISON

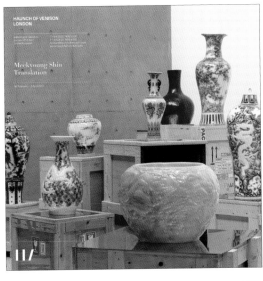

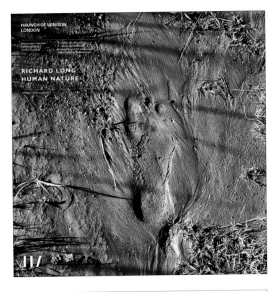

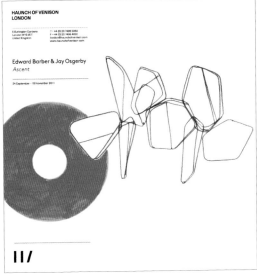

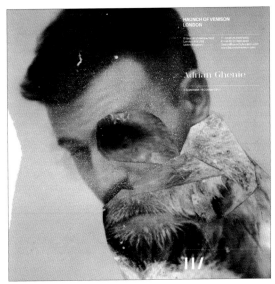

Home House

One of central London's secret gems, Home House brings together people of all cultures, offering its members a unique place in which to network, relax and party.

Spanning three townhouses designed by architect James Wyatt in 1773, the discreet Georgian exteriors of Portman Square's Home House conceal a glorious juxtaposition of interior design styles: Robert Adam's neoclassical opulence, renowned architect Zaha Hadid's sensual, sculptural furnishings and the superior detail of 'superdesigners' Candy & Candy. Frequently hosting members' events and parties, the House is a truly glamorous venue for any type of celebration or occasion.

homehouse.co.uk

Hunter

For more than 150 years, Hunter has merged functionality, fashion and true British style. The result? High quality footwear that excels in any environment.

Specialising in authentic, contemporary footwear and accessories, Hunter is about timeless British style. Designed to be outstanding in any field, from city streets to music festivals and rugged countryside, Hunter footwear is recognised for its performance, durability and comfort – achieved through a fusion of tradition and technology. Worn by fashion-savvy men and women worldwide, the Hunter Original boot is firmly established as a style classic.

hunter-boot.com

HUNTER

Illamasqua

Renowned for its uncompromising dedication to self-expression, cult British beauty brand Illamasqua has revitalised the make-up industry, firmly establishing itself as a serious international player.

Launched in 2008 as the brainchild of founder Julian Kynaston and marketing agency Propaganda, Illamasqua has created a super-strain of professional make-up that resonates emotionally with the consumer. With a top team, including make-up artist Alex Box and Agent Provocateur founder Joseph Corré, the independent beauty brand has gained a cult following with avant-garde imagery that transcends the expectations of the beauty industry, and is now available in more than 100 outlets globally.

illamasqua.com

ILLAMASQUA
Make-up for your alter ego

Jägermeister

A secret blend of 56 herbs, blossoms, roots and fruits creates the truly unique taste of Jägermeister, which should always be served ice cold.

Developed more than 75 years ago, Jägermeister's unique character is conjured up by the perfect combination of pure, natural ingredients and the skill of its master distillers. The herbal liqueur is matured in an oak barrel for up to a year, with 383 quality-control checks ensuring its complex taste is flawless. Always served ice cold, either as a shot or with a mixer, Jägermeister has secured a place at the heart of festivals, events and parties worldwide.

jagermeister.co.uk

Jägermeister
SERVE ICE COLD

Jelly Belly

First cooked up in 1976, Jelly Belly® beans burst with Really Real™ flavours that delight taste buds the world over. The genius is in the recipe.

Full of true-to-life flavour, Jelly Belly® is The Original Gourmet Jelly Bean®. Developed for the sophisticated palate, the beans are packed with intensely juicy taste, from their brightly coloured shells right through to their centres, and can take up to 21 days to create. The 90 authentic flavours use natural ingredients such as chocolate, coconut, fruit juices and purées wherever possible, and can be combined to create an almost infinite number of taste experiences.

jellybelly-uk.com

John Lewis

John Lewis is renowned for its inspiring range of quality products and unique customer service, delivered by friendly experts who are also Partners in the business.

Britain's favourite multichannel retailer, John Lewis has earned its place in shoppers' hearts and minds through its enduring customer commitment – to be Never Knowingly Undersold, on quality, price and service. As a partnership there's admiration for operating a different business model where every Partner serves you as though they own the company, because they do.

johnlewis.com

John Lewis

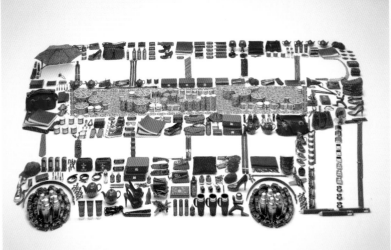

Kiss

World-famous Kiss connects millions of passionate dance, hip hop and R&B fans each week via radio, TV, social media and mobile phones.

As an established entertainment brand, Kiss has one mission: 'never stand still'. Available across the UK, Kiss presents the latest in music from the famous and discovered, to the fresh but yet to be uncovered. It's about celebrity and lifestyle, and it's on the pulse of all things trending. Kiss is an iconic and dynamic name respected by artists, audiences and advertisers alike. 'Music is Life' to Kiss and its four million young consumers.

totalkiss.com

Last.fm

Last.fm is the world's leading personalised radio service, using the music tastes of millions of listeners around the world to connect them with artists and live events they'll love.

Last.fm kick-started the UK's digital economy back in 2005, when London's 'Silicon Roundabout' was still known as Old Street. Today it's the leader in personalised radio and social music online. Through a process known as 'scrobbling', users effortlessly track the music they listen to. They can scrobble from more than 600 different media players, accessing recommendations for new artists, live events, festivals and much more with every song they play.

last.fm

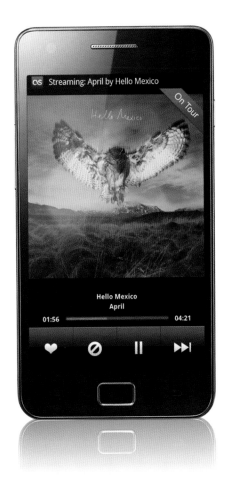

Lavazza

A blend of 115 years' experience, Italian authenticity, incredible passion and sharp innovation makes Lavazza an icon for espresso excellence around the world.

Lavazza's range of espresso machines combines the latest in technology with the true passion of Italian coffee culture. Its aim: to bring an authentic and evocative espresso experience to coffee drinkers worldwide. With a belief that coffee can only be made 'my way' – the 'A MODO MIO' philosophy – Lavazza develops products that together create the perfect cup of coffee. Launched in September 2011, the new AEG range is its latest innovation.

lavazzamodomio.co.uk

Le Gavroche

Respected and influential, Michel Roux Jr's Michelin-starred Mayfair restaurant has played a leading role in shaping the UK's gastronomic landscape.

Opened in 1967 by the Roux brothers, Le Gavroche sets the impeccable standards of cooking and service by which others are judged. Since taking over the reins from his father Albert in 1991, chef patron Michel Roux Jr has prepared dishes that ensure the highest of reputations is maintained among diners and critics. Over the last 40 years, the experience of dining at Le Gavroche has remained synonymous with timeless excellence.

le-gavroche.co.uk

Liberty

As one of London's most loved and unique retail emporiums, Liberty has earned its reputation as an iconic destination store.

Since it first opened its doors in 1875, Liberty has established itself as a cutting-edge luxury emporium where the finest meets the rarest from around the world. The exquisite Tudor-revival building in the heart of the Regent Street shopping district has been Liberty's much-loved home since the 1920s, stocking today's most sought-after fashion, design and beauty brands.

liberty.co.uk

Manolo Blahnik

For almost 40 years, Manolo Blahnik's designs have conveyed the very essence of precision, balance and luxury. 'Shoes,' he says, 'help transform a woman.'

One of the world's most influential footwear designers, Manolo Blahnik has spellbound an international set of adoring and loyal devotees with his exquisitely crafted shoes. From his distinctive theatrical sketches – which have become as coveted as the shoes themselves – through to the precision workmanship that creates every silhouette, Blahnik perfects each design with his own hands. Individual works of art, Blahnik's shoes have been celebrated both in print and at London's Design Museum.

manoloblahnik.com

MANOLO BLAHNIK

Marmite

Love it or hate it, Marmite is firmly entrenched in the British consciousness, and the sticky stuff's cult appeal has given rise to a plethora of merchandise.

Marmite is a true British institution, 109 years old and counting, and its iconic Love/Hate campaign has created a loyal band of fanatical Marmite 'Lovers'. A leading savoury spread, Marmite has annual sales of approximately £46 million, while the huge popularity of the brand with its uniquely divisive taste provides it with hundreds of free mentions in the press each year.

marmite.com

Maybelline New York

The aim of Maybelline is to empower women to make a new statement by exploring new looks, experimenting without risk, and flaunting their own artistry.

Maybelline reflects the attitude, style and energy of New York. Innovative and forward-thinking, the brand introduces the most advanced technologies and revolutionary products, having even invented the first mascara in 1915. Inspired by the runway, it creates the latest shades and on-trend colours while remaining accessible and affordable. Maybelline offers high-performance products in more than 129 countries worldwide.

maybelline.co.uk

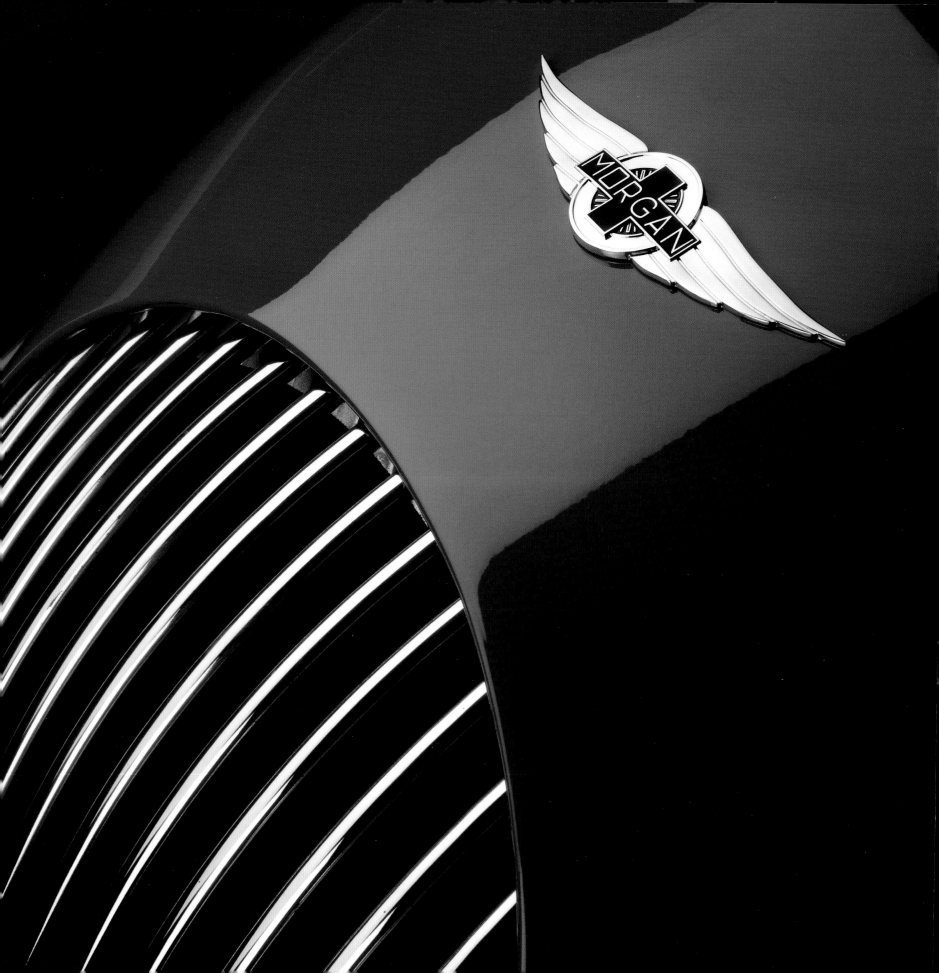

Morgan

A fusion of old and new, Morgan's handcrafted cars are true British icons that combine classic design with 21st-century technology.

Founded on the success of its famous Three-Wheeler, Morgan's illustrious history spans more than a century of bespoke manufacture, using traditional coach-building techniques alongside modern engineering. Its philosophy to create motor cars that are pure, elegant, light and fast has brought us modern-day icons such as the Morgan Classic range and the relaunched Morgan 3 Wheeler, while the Eva GT concept car and the limited run Aero SuperSports are the ultimate in lightweight luxury.

morgan-motor.co.uk

I AM A SPLASH OF COLOUR

Nikon

As an iconic global brand, Nikon has been making first-class cameras and lenses for over 90 years. Always at the heart of the image, Nikon makes quality pictures achievable for everyone.

Perfection, innovation, passion and fun. Nikon is all of these things. As one of the world's leading photographic equipment manufacturers, Nikon produces award-winning imaging products, from easy-to-use compact digital cameras to professional DSLRs and lenses, which inspire creativity and set the highest standards in photography. Nikon's 'I AM NIKON' campaign, and its continued sponsorship of C4's Hollyoaks, has helped to raise awareness of its COOLPIX compact cameras among a younger, mass-market audience.

nikon.co.uk

At the heart of the image

Original Penguin

Original Penguin may have made its mark in the 1950s, but it is still turning heads today – by keeping one fashionable foot in the past, and an eye on the future.

Known for its kitsch prints and irreverent wit, Original Penguin first caught the attention of fashion-savvy men back in 1955 with its hugely successful golf polo shirt. But there's more to the brand than meets the eye: it's a combination of retro flair and subtle branding, endorsed by celebrities and embraced by the everyman. The look is classic yet casual, sold all over the world, but found in only the most select stores.

originalpenguin.eu

Power Plate

Sophisticated design combined with groundbreaking technology and unrivalled performance makes Power Plate the global leader in Acceleration Training™ products.

Founded in 2000 by Dutch Olympic trainer Guus van der Meer, Power Plate has revolutionised 21st-century fitness culture with its unique vibration training equipment. Favoured by celebrities, sports professionals and everyday users alike – from Hollywood star Mark Wahlberg to Rebecca Romero, Britain's Beijing Olympic champion – the medically certified products have garnered a devoted following by enhancing the effects of exercise to deliver faster results, whether at home or in the gym.

powerplate.com/uk

Prada

With an enviable reputation for luxury ready-to-wear that exudes elegance and a touch of the unexpected, Prada is a leading force in fashion.

One of the world's most prestigious fashion and luxury goods brands, Prada is synonymous with almost a century of innovative and modern design. Under the vision of Miuccia Prada, the label has become known for its covetable collections of accessories and ready-to-wear, characterised by exceptional craftsmanship and alluringly unorthodox detailing. Sensational shows and stores designed by innovative architects complete Prada's all-encompassing creative vision, and bring the brand's sense of theatre to life.

prada.com

PRADA

Pret A Manger

Pret A Manger creates handmade, natural food, avoiding the obscure chemicals, additives and preservatives found in much of the 'prepared' and 'fast' food on the market today.

For 25 years, Pret has kept quality, service and people at the heart of its business. Nearly all Pret shops have their own kitchen, where the sandwiches, salads and wraps are handmade from freshly prepared ingredients. Food that is unsold at the end of the day is offered to charities to help feed the homeless. Pret has 230 shops in the UK and a growing business in New York, Washington DC, Chicago and Hong Kong.

pret.com

Proud

**With an unrivalled identity
in the world of music and
photography, the iconic Proud
brand comprises some of
London's finest venues combining
culture and entertainment.**

Founded by Alex Proud in 1998, Proud Galleries launched
as a groundbreaking gallery bringing accessible rock'n'roll
photography to the masses. Now spanning three photography
galleries, two live music venues and two vaudevillian Supper
Clubs as well as a relaxed diner, the Proud name stands at the
pinnacle of London's arts and music scene. Proud's latest venture
sees the reinvention of the superclub with Proud2 at The O2.

proud.co.uk

ESCAPE

ART

VILLAS

BESPOKE

QUBE

COMMUNICATIONS

ESTATES

COVERED

AEROSPEED

GIFTS

MUSIC

WINE

CONCIERGE

EVENTS

FLOWERS

PUBLISHING

DRIVEN

GROUP

TRAVEL

EDUCATION

QUIVERZ

DESIGN

SOHO

ONE

PORTLAND PLACE

iQ

TV

VIAVI

AVIATION

WEDDINGS

FOUNDATION

EPICURE

QENSU

HOME

NATURAL

Quintessentially

As the world's leading luxury lifestyle group and private members club, Quintessentially provides its members with a unique, global concierge service, on hand 24/7/365.

With more than 60 offices around the world and 32 sister businesses covering every facet of the luxury sphere, a Quintessentially membership is your passport to a world of privilege and style. Whether you need a last-minute table at New York's hottest restaurant, VIP tickets to the latest premiere, or that must-have Birkin to finish your collection, Quintessentially will access the inaccessible on your behalf. Welcome to the wonderful world of Quintessentially.

quintessentiallygroup.com

QUINTESSENTIALLY
GROUP

2011/12
CoolBrands.uk.com

Royal Opera House

An international cultural icon, the Royal Opera House is uncompromising in its creative and artistic ambition to be the best.

The Royal Opera House is a resource for the nation and an international symbol of excellence: the home of world-class performance, a hub for innovation and experimentation, and the base for an extensive programme of education that encourages creativity and self-discovery through engagement with the arts. It is home to The Royal Ballet, The Royal Opera, ROH2, the Orchestra of the Royal Opera House and the Royal Opera Chorus.

roh.org.uk

Salty Dog

Made from the best potatoes, thickly sliced and cooked in their skins in pure sunflower oil, Salty Dog crisps 'bite back' thanks to their crunch and 100 per cent real seasonings.

Salty Dog bucks the trend of most hand-cooked artisan crisps. It uses the best ingredients but doesn't make a big deal about it – because the quality speaks for itself. Tantalising the nation's taste buds since the brand was born in 2003, Salty Dog is the product of Dave and Judy Willis's enterprising spirit, its name an affectionate nod to their faithful dog Ruby.

saltydog-grrr.com

Shaun Leane

Internationally celebrated for pushing the boundaries of jewellery design, Shaun Leane is evolving from an individual artist-jeweller into a trailblazing luxury jewellery house.

From his beginnings in a traditional English workshop, focusing on diamond mounting and antique restoration, Shaun Leane has taken the fashion world by storm with his darkly romantic and beautifully crafted jewellery. Alongside his themed collections and bespoke pieces, Leane has also designed iconic catwalk jewels for the likes of Givenchy and the late Alexander McQueen. His work has been described by prestigious London auction house Sotheby's as 'antiques of the future'.

shaunleane.com

SHAUNLEANE

Main image: designed by Shaun Leane & Daphne Guinness. Smaller images: photography by Chris Moore

SHAZAM PARTNERS WITH OLD NAVY TO CREATE A FUN, FRESH, SHOPPING EXPERIENCE

Shazam

As the world's leading mobile discovery company, Shazam enables consumers to experience and share content across mobile devices and the internet.

Shazam has evolved into one of the world's most recognised brands. With more than 150 million Shazamers in 200 countries, Shazam has created a new way for people to learn more about the music, TV shows and brands they love and share their finds with friends. With Shazam, people can discover, buy and share music and unlock content from their favourite shows and commercials.

shazam.com

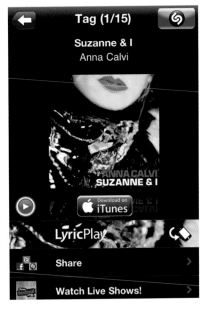

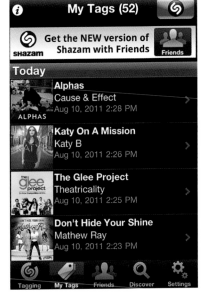

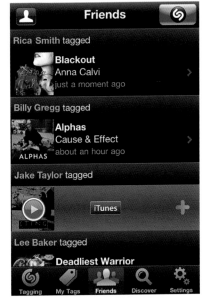

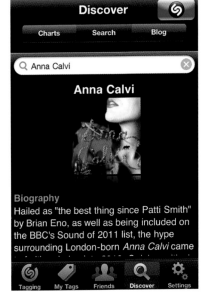

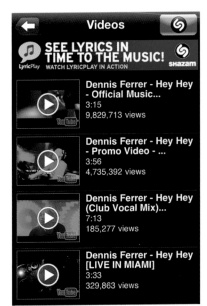

STELLA ARTOIS

She is a thing of beauty

Stella Artois

An international icon of brewing craftsmanship and tradition, Stella Artois is the world's best-selling Belgian beer.

Stella Artois exclusively blends 600 years of brewing tradition with the finest ingredients to produce an unequalled beer taste. The brand has an unceasing commitment to setting the highest standards, from its uniquely crafted chalice that preserves the quality of the beer, to its World Draught Quality programme, educating bartenders worldwide. The result is a jewel among beers, faultlessly poured and presented, for those who settle for nothing less than the most refined perfection.

stellaartois.com

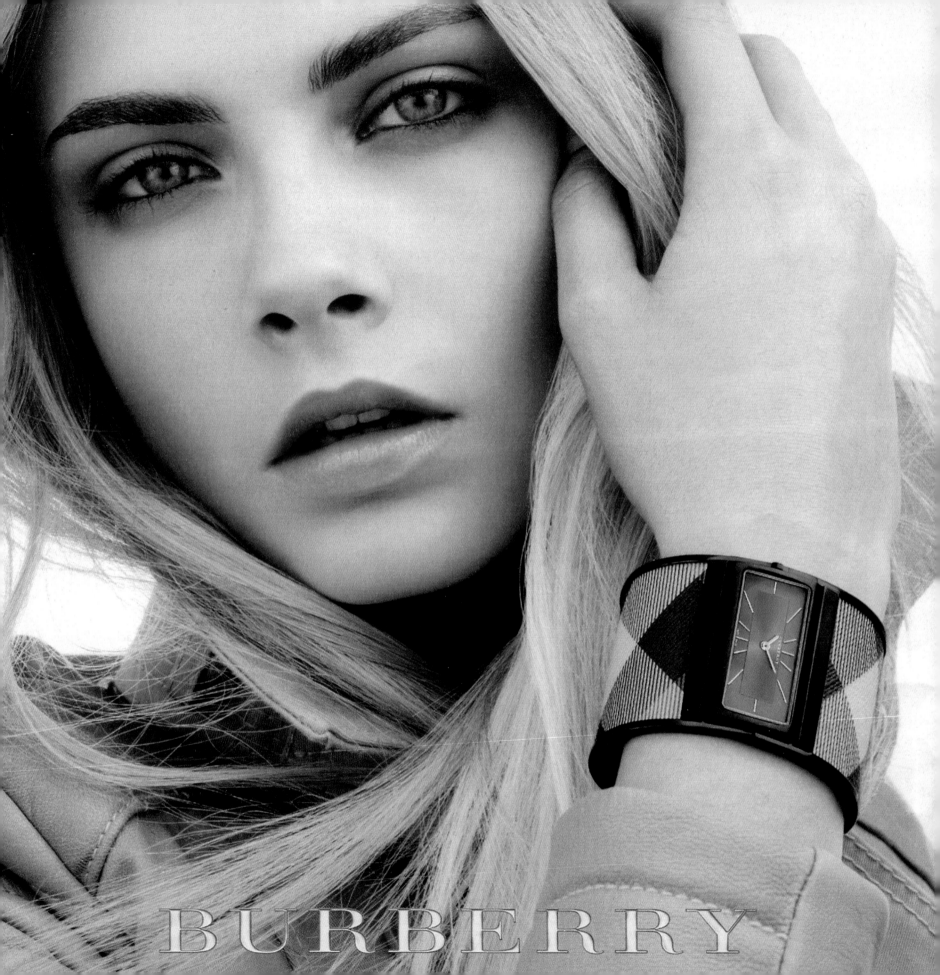

BURBERRY

Storm

Launching the careers of numerous defining individuals of recent times, Storm is a major player in a fashion industry facing new challenges and opportunities in this digital age.

Storm model management has over 22 years' experience discovering and developing the careers of some of fashion's most famous faces. Offering expert guidance and fostering longevity based on talent and integrity, Storm has cultivated a client list that includes Kate Moss, Lily Cole, Cindy Crawford, Eva Herzigova, Jourdan Dunn, Alex Wek and Cara Delevingne. Storm expanded its philosophy by establishing a Special Bookings Division that provides commercial opportunities for talent including Emma Watson, Bip Ling, Lily Allen and Tom Aikens.

stormmodels.com

storm

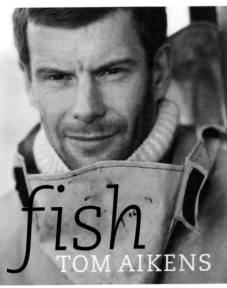

Images: Mario Testino, Mert & Marcus, Matt Erwin, John Lawrence-Jones and Cristian Barnett

Sunseeker

Over the decades that Sunseeker has been building its distinctive luxury motor yachts, it has evolved into a true icon, becoming the ultimate lifestyle statement.

A truly global leader in the design and build of luxury motor yachts, Sunseeker exports to more than 61 countries and is widely recognised as the pre-eminent luxury marine brand in the world today. A brand with enormous global strength, part of its success lies in the commitment to constantly set new standards and benchmarks. Creating a range of craft, from 43ft to 131ft, Sunseeker prides itself on continuous design, innovation and style.

sunseeker.com

The May Fair

If it's happening in London, it's happening at The May Fair – an icon of expressive design with a playful, progressive style that redefines the ethos of five-star hospitality.

Its glamorous heritage, bold design and distinctive style make The May Fair Hotel a true one-off. Imbued with the energy of its London location, The May Fair is a collection of experiences – including Quince, a luxe Eastern Mediterranean eatery with a modern take on one of the world's oldest cuisines, and 150, an exclusive magnum bar bristling with rare pleasures. Dramatic without compromising on comfort, with service that anticipates but never assumes, The May Fair redefines modern luxury with playful panache.

themayfairhotel.co.uk

THE MAY FAIR
HOTEL

The North Face

Technical apparel and equipment brand The North Face is the premier producer of innovative expedition and outdoor gear, driven by the tenet Never Stop Exploring.

Since 1968, The North Face has grown beyond its origins in climbing to bring passionately designed, technically superior outdoor apparel, equipment and footwear to anyone who walks, runs, cycles, camps, travels, climbs or slides on snow. Fuelled by the principle Never Stop Exploring, The North Face unites product with athletes, vision with possibility, to encourage adventure, outdoor exploration and an active lifestyle.

thenorthface.com

NEVER STOP EXPLORING

Main image: athlete Hervé Barmasse, photographer Damiano Levati. Smaller image: athlete Johann Jonsson, photographer Oskar Enander

The Wapping Project

Now in its 11th year, The Wapping Project is celebrated for its singular combination of challenging contemporary art and performance, fine food and inspiring architecture.

The Wapping Project is housed in Wapping Hydraulic Power Station, on the north bank of the Thames. The modern architecture identifies with the beauty of the historic building, which dates back to 1890, and aims to create a backdrop against which artists can create audacious, contemporary work. All pieces are new, commissioned and site-specific, frequently touring internationally. The Wapping Project has achieved international cult status among architects, artists and lovers of great food alike.

thewappingproject.com

Main image: Yohji Making Waves, 2011. Smaller image: The Wapping Project, photographer Angus Boulton

Tiger Beer

First brewed in Singapore in 1932, Tiger Beer embarked on a journey that has seen it go from strength to strength, becoming one of the world's favourite international premium beers.

Tiger Beer is quickly establishing itself as a beer for the discerning consumer. In 2011/12, the brand's 'Know The Not Known' integrated campaign reflects the essence of the beer, inviting engagement from old and new admirers. In collaboration with pioneering creative talent in the fields of design, film and music, and with digital at its heart, Tiger seeks to reward those who show their curiosity in the detail of the campaign with exclusive access to rich online content and exclusive events.

facebook.com/tigerbeeruk

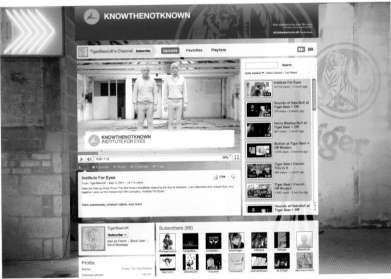

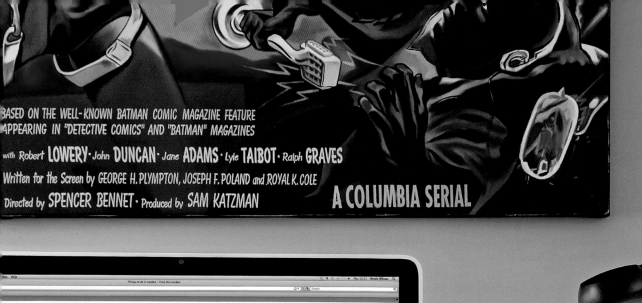

Time Out Guides

Time Out: the indispensable guide to what's happening in the most exciting places on the planet, written by local experts connected to the very best of their city.

Time Out is an international multimedia producer of cultural experiences for urban adventurers. Its currency is independent, up-to-date information to help users remain at the cutting edge of culture. Time Out guidebooks, e-books and apps, alongside TimeOut.com, live events and magazines, offer everything needed to get the best from a place. Time Out is the official publisher of travel and tourism guides for the London 2012 Olympic Games and Paralympic Games.

timeout.com

Top Trumps

An irresistible combination of discovery, competition and fun makes Top Trumps the world's most popular card game.

Since its rebirth in 1999, more than 70 million packs of Top Trumps have been sold around the globe. Through a cool mixture of facts, stats, imagery and the world's hottest licenses, the game is always evolving. This evolution has now gone digital with the arrival of the Top Trumps Collection App and the Top Trumps Live! game for the web. As for the kids – the current national Top Trumps Tournament schools champion is Jack Dyson!

toptrumps.com

Virgin Media: TiVo® Service.

Virgin Media

The first company to cater for all of its customers' digital needs, Virgin Media is purpose built for the way digital media is consumed today.

Providing broadband, TV, phone and mobile services to almost 12 million UK homes, Virgin Media owns the UK's largest fibre optic network, delivers the fastest broadband and was first to offer customers a complete digital package. Recently launching a groundbreaking television service in partnership with TiVo, the brand continues to break down digital boundaries and subscribes to the belief that customers should have access to content across multiple devices, at home and out and about.

virginmedia.com

wagamama

Combining fresh and nutritious food with friendly service and value for money, wagamama remains strong in its belief of the balance of 'positive eating + positive living'.

With the opening of its first restaurant in London's Bloomsbury in 1992, wagamama unleashed a new dining experience. A pioneer of the now popular bench-style seating, wagamama led the way with electronic ordering and a unique food offering. Today it has restaurants in 17 countries, has evolved its brand to include a retail range of cookbooks and sauces, launched an iPhone app which lets you order takeout, and has introduced the wagamama lounge to satisfy festival-goers.

wagamama.com

wagamama

WAH Nails

With a philosophy to hand paint 'whatever you want on your fingertips', WAH has earned its reputation as the original home of nail art.

WAH started life in 2005 as a fanzine – championing cool, talented girls that were making waves on the creative scene. It quickly spawned a loyal online following, creating an international 'downtown girls' community and instigating the arrival of the WAH Nails salon. Since opening its Dalston doors in August 2009, the salon has pioneered the concept of nail art as a beauty norm. Over the past year alone, WAH has painted nails for everyone from catwalk stars to girls in classic cars.

wah-nails.com

Wonderbra

Famed for its attention-grabbing campaigns, Wonderbra is the leader in push-up bra innovation. Boosting women's confidence as well as their cleavage, it's the ultimate fashion solution.

Always a brand to stand out from the crowd, Wonderbra markets its lingerie with the same innovative and uplifting approach that inspires its bra designs, from its iconic Hello Boys campaign though to its latest traffic-stopping 3D Full Effect billboard. Its '100 Ways' Multiplunge bra and the unique technology of Ultimate Strapless ignited a revolution in lingerie solutions, while a collaboration with burlesque artiste Dita Von Teese brought Wonderbra sultry glamour to the high street.

wonderbra.co.uk

HELLO BOYS.

THE ORIGINAL PUSH-UP PLUNGE BRA. AVAILABLE IN SIZES 32-38 ABC.

Experience the Full Effect

Xbox

Xbox 360 enjoyed its biggest ever year in 2010, with the launch of Kinect for Xbox 360 taking games and entertainment to new levels in extraordinary new ways.

Xbox 360 continues to redefine entertainment in the home, with the evolution of Xbox LIVE – now a complete entertainment system encompassing voice-activated search, live TV, HD movies, social networking and multiplayer gaming. Xbox remains the biggest and best platform for traditional gamers, with blockbuster titles including Gears of War 3 launching in 2011. Kinect for Xbox 360 titles are also set to launch in partnership with entertainment giants LucasArts, Disney and Sesame Street.

facebook.com/xboxuk

YMC

Inspired by a modernist and functional approach to design, YMC creates timeless clothing that allows individuals to carve out their own style: You Must Create.

Established in London in 1995 by Fraser Moss and Jimmy Collins, YMC was formed in response to the demand for stylish, yet functional, modern clothing. With an ethos inspired by Raymond Loewy, a pioneer of American industrial design who believed that 'you must create your own design style', the brand is influenced not by seasonal trends but by an aim to provide intelligent clothing that is both wearable and distinctive.

youmustcreate.com

YMC

Expert Council
2011/12

In these ever-changing times, what, exactly, constitutes 'cool'?
At the core of the 2011/12 CoolBrands® decision-making process are 36 council members – style leaders, media movers and shakers and creative thinkers – who are all perfectly placed to answer that question.

Chairman, CoolBrands®
Expert Council

Stephen Cheliotis
Chief Executive, The Centre for Brand Analysis (TCBA)

In 2007, Stephen founded TCBA, which offers specialist research and insight to brand owners and marketing agencies, and works with a range of business-to-consumer and business-to-business clients. He also speaks at events worldwide on branding issues and comments on branding for the international media.

Adam Laycock

Walé Adeyemi MBE
Fashion Designer

One of the UK's most successful fashion
designers and an A-list stylist, Walé is
a proud Prince's Trust Ambassador, and
in 2008 was awarded an MBE for his services
to fashion. 2011 saw Walé show at Nigeria
Fashion Week, and expand his range to
include limited-edition design collaborations
of home and lifestyle accessories.

Kate Creasey
Former Editor,
Cosmopolitan.co.uk

Kate is an award-winning online journalist
and became editor of Cosmopolitan.co.uk
in November 2007, remaining at its helm
until June 2011. With more than 10 years'
experience as an online editor, Kate is an
authority on web trends and online publishing.

Rob da Bank
DJ & Bestival Founder

Rob da Bank is a British club DJ, BBC Radio 1
broadcaster and the founder and curator of
the multi-award-winning Bestival festivals.
Rob also founded independent record label
Sunday Best in 1995, and has since propelled
Dan Le Sac Vs Scroobius Pip and teenage
rockabillies Kitty, Daisy & Lewis into the charts.

'Success can be the biggest challenge to keeping cool
– brands like Apple have managed to keep their cool
credentials despite their global success by constantly
innovating, staying true to their philosophies and always
managing to be aspirational.' **Kate Creasey**

Ben de Lisi
Fashion Designer

Ben has a long-standing couture business, which he has shown at London Fashion Week, and is famous for dressing Kate Winslet for the Oscars and other red-carpet events. He has designed diffusion lines for Debenhams since 1997, spanning home, womenswear and accessories, most recently reviving the Principles brand for relaunch in 2010.

James-lee Duffy
Art Director, Graphic Designer & Illustrator, We Are Shadows

James-lee is six foot six inches of art director, designer and artist, and has worked on brands such as She Died Of Beauty, Nintendo, Coca-Cola, Appletiser and Diageo. His illustration work has shown in New York, Japan, London and Scandinavia and his art zine 'Pavement Licker' is found in cities across the world.

Gizzi Erskine
TV Chef

Top chef Gizzi is a leading light in the crossover between food and style. Best known for presenting Channel 4's Cook Yourself Thin, she has since gone on to publish the hugely successful book, Gizzi's Kitchen Magic, as well as fronting C4's Cookery School with Michelin-starred chef Richard Corrigan.

Sadie Frost
Actress & Fashion Designer

Kate Halfpenny
Fashion Designer & Stylist

**Ruby Hammer MBE &
Millie Kendall MBE**
Founders,
Ruby & Millie

Sadie recently played the lead in the film Animal Charm and is also writing and producing several short features. In fashion, her award-winning label FrostFrench is introducing a new line in Debenhams, Iris & Edie, alongside its established Floozie range. Sadie is also launching her own skincare line in spring 2012.

Kate is a celebrity fashion stylist and designer, famed for her bespoke creations and for working with the likes of Rihanna, Daisy Lowe, Erin O'Connor, Emilia Fox and Kate Moss. She also creates costumes for brand giants such as PlayStation, Moschino and Hugo Boss.

The eponymous Ruby & Millie brand launched in 1998, drawing on the duo's wealth of experience in the beauty industry. Ruby, an international make-up artist, and internationally successful beauty publicist Millie, were both awarded an MBE in 2007.

'A brand needs to stay on top of consumers' demands in order to keep its cool status, to evolve with the times, to stay ahead of the game.'
Kate Halfpenny

Newby Hands
Associate Editor & Director
of Health & Beauty,
Harper's Bazaar

Newby was Style & Beauty editor at the Daily
Mail before moving to Harper's Bazaar 13 years
ago. In 2008 she was named Beauty Journalist
of the Year at the P&G Beauty Awards.

Rickie Haywood-Williams & Melvin Odoom
Hosts,
Kiss Breakfast Show

Rickie and Melvin host the award-winning
Kiss 100 Breakfast Show every weekday
morning. The presenting duo are also
known from their long-serving relationship
with MTV, having fronted shows for the
channel over several years.

Kelly Hoppen MBE
Designer

A world-renowned British designer, Kelly
designs apartments, houses and yachts for an
international private client list and undertakes
commercial design projects including hotels,
restaurants, offices and aircraft interiors. She
also shares her knowledge and style secrets via
the Kelly Hoppen Design School, and designs
ranges of home furnishings and accessories.

'Coolness for me is something that
gives me the I-need-this-in-my-life
feeling.' **Kelly Hoppen**

Jessie J
Music Artist

Brit Award-winning Jessie has sold an astonishing half a million copies of her number-two debut platinum-selling album. Nobody's Perfect, released in May 2011, saw Jessie secure her third consecutive Top 10 UK single, and she has had over 150 million views on YouTube.

Jo Jackson
Managing Director,
'i-am' beyond

Former co-founder of the award-winning fashion boutique Beyond the Valley, Jo now consults for the likes of Nokia, Diageo, Bestseller and my-wardrobe. Her marketing agency with 'i-am' associates specialises in building brand advocacy, innovative strategies and events for established and emerging fashion and lifestyle brands the world over.

Dolly Jones
Editor,
VOGUE.COM

Dolly became a writer at VOGUE.COM in 2000. She rose to editor in 2005 and leads the trusted authority on fashion, which incorporates a daily news service and coverage of every catwalk show in the world.

'Cool brands have one foot in the now, and one foot in the future. They are relevant today, but inspirational with the promise to always offer us something we want to own or want to be a part of. Cool brands inspire future cool brands. It's an evolution.' **Hannah Marshall**

Daisy Knights
Jewellery Designer

Daisy's striking jewellery designs have propelled her to the forefront of the industry. Her pieces have been included in many high-end fashion publications and have been worn by celebrities including Alexa Chung, Daisy Lowe and Laura Bailey.

Mark Krendel
Partnerships Director,
Universal Music Group UK

Mark has spent more than 12 years at the cutting edge of the music industry, and has been instrumental in digital and commercial projects for Jive, Polydor and Universal. He has delivered multi-platform campaigns for the likes of the Black Eyed Peas and Take That, and sealed partnerships with brands such as Burberry and Coca-Cola.

Lee Lapthorne
Fashion & Creative Director

Lee is one of the country's leading fashion and event-management experts, and a designer. He is the founder and director of Doll and On|Off, and has worked with clients such as Gucci, CKOne, Pam Hogg, Jessie J, Preen, Louise Gray, Italian Vogue, BBC, ITV, P&G and Range Rover.

Rankin

Hannah Marshall
Designer

Since founding her eponymous luxury fashion label in 2007, Hannah has established herself internationally as a designer and entrepreneur. Credited with reinventing the (Little) Black Dress, Hannah Marshall encapsulates body-conscious and dynamic silhouettes engineered with intelligent precision. Her designs are worn by Florence Welch, Janet Jackson and Jessica Alba, to name a few.

Zara Martin
TV Presenter & Model

Zara is known for her great sense of style and for presenting The LICK with Trevor Nelson on MTV. She also fronts her own show on Current TV, Zara's Show, and presents backstage at the GLAMOUR Awards.

Liz Matthews
Entertainment Publicist

Liz is an entertainment publicist with more than a decade of experience and a client list including cover stars Alexa Chung, Rosie Huntington-Whiteley, Alfie Allen, Maxine Peake, Daisy Lowe and Laura Bailey. A former journalist with an enviable list of contacts, Liz also consults for brands across fashion, film and music.

Kay McMahon
Digital Director,
Wallpaper*

Kay has been at global design authority
Wallpaper* magazine since 2007 and
has overseen wallpaper.com's traffic
growth and expansion onto new platforms.
Prior to Wallpaper*, she worked in online
media, advertising and broadcasting,
and is a wedding DJ in her spare time.

Natasha McNamara
Editor,
GLAMOUR.com

Natasha started her career working on film
magazines, but found her passion to be in
digital publishing, where she has been working
across lifestyle and fashion websites for the
past five years. Editing GLAMOUR.com,
she combines her love of celebrity, fashion
and shopping with her obsession for digital
strategy and developing brands online.

James Murphy
Founding Partner,
adam&eve

James founded adam&eve, a new-wave
creative agency, three years ago. Since launch,
its work has been lauded and awarded across
clients such as John Lewis, Foster's, Phones
4u and Save the Children. adam&eve was
named Creative Agency of the Year 2010 by
both Campaign and Marketing magazines.

'Something that creates a feeling of admiration or
desire can be considered 'cool' – it's such a subjective
term, but transcends generations to imply appreciation
on some level.' **Kay McMahon**

Miquita Oliver
Broadcaster

Steve Parkinson
Managing Director, Kiss

Paul Percival & Adam Reed
Managing Director / Creative
Director, Percy & Reed

Broadcaster Miquita has spent the past 10 years hosting Channel 4 youth strand T4, having first hit our screens on music show Popworld with Simon Amstell.

Steve has been at the helm of dance and R&B radio and TV brand Kiss for five years. Originally a London pirate station, Kiss now broadcasts across the UK on radio, TV and online, and continues to reinvent itself to appeal to new music fans in a digital age.

Percy & Reed is London's most talked about salon. Renowned for artistry, passion and technique, Paul and Adam have a devoted fashion and A-list following, not only in the salon environment, but backstage at London Fashion Week and on the red carpet.

'It needs integrity, it needs to really stand for something and stick to it, no matter what the trend. True cool transcends fashion, and for a brand to achieve that it needs real bravery because it will be sailing against the wind. Cool doesn't care what other people think.' **Stuart Semple**

Way Perry
Fashion Director,
Man About Town

Danny Sangra
Artist, Art Director
& Designer

Stuart Semple
Artist

An editor and creative director for fashion and style magazines Wonderland, Rollacoaster and Man About Town, Way also works worldwide styling shows for the likes of Katie Eary and Frankie Morello, as well as celebrities such as Professor Green, Jessie J and Pharrell Williams. His own menswear label is due for launch in 2012.

A polymath of creativity, Danny incorporates design, film, illustration and video/art direction. He's had solo exhibitions in London, Europe, Tokyo and New York, and worked/collaborated with clients such as Sony, Marc by Marc Jacobs, SHOWstudio and V Magazine. He has also launched his own knitwear collection, AMS.

Stuart has achieved critical acclaim as a provocative image-maker, social commentator and visual spokesperson. He exhibits worldwide, curates for leading institutions and writes for national publications. The opening of his most recent solo exhibition, The Happy House at Morton Metropolis, London, was broadcast live on the BBC.

Lisa Snowdon
Presenter, Model & Co-Host, Capital Breakfast Show

As well as being one of the UK's top models of recent years, Lisa has also carved out a successful career in radio and television. She currently co-hosts the Capital Breakfast Show with Johnny Vaughan, while her most recent TV work includes hosting four series of Britain's Next Top Model for Living.

Tim Soar
Menswear & Womenswear Designer

Since Tim launched his eponymous menswear label in 2005, success has continued apace. His showcases are now popular fixtures at London Fashion Week, while Autumn/ Winter 2011 sees the launch of his first full womenswear collection. Tim also founded Music Concrete, producing music for events hosted by brands such as Prada, Levi's and The Great Eastern Hotel.

Anna-Marie Solowij
Beauty Journalist & Brand Consultant

Anna-Marie is an award-winning beauty journalist. Formerly beauty director of British Vogue, she remains a contributing editor there while also writing for the FT's How To Spend It and Condé Nast Traveller. She also utilises her beauty expertise as a partner in the brand development company Rain 23.

'The definition of 'cool' has changed. It used to be anything that wasn't overexposed. In the age of the global brand, cool status is gained for (almost) opposite reasons.' **Anna-Marie Solowij**

Nadja Swarovski
VP International
Communications & Creative
Director, Swarovski

Nadja has elevated the venerable crystal empire to the cutting edge of 21st-century fashion, jewellery and lighting design. In 2000, Nadja set up offices in London, LA and New York to work with and nurture both emerging and established design talent, including Alexander McQueen, Karl Lagerfeld, Christopher Kane, Tord Boontje, Ron Arad and Zaha Hadid.

Jo Tutchener
Founder,
Beauty Seen PR

Jo launched Beauty Seen PR (part of the Exposure group) in 2007. The agency provides dynamic campaigns to brands such as Cowshed, Topshop Make-Up, NARS, Decléor and Revlon, as well as creating spas backstage at events such as The Brit Awards and MTV EMAs.

Grace Woodward
TV Presenter & Stylist

Grace is best known as a judge on Britain's Next Top Model and former Head of Fashion on The X Factor. She is also an award-winning stylist in the fashion industry, having styled covers for The Sunday Times' Style magazine, as well as the esteemed GQ Men of the Year cover.

'To gain cool status, the brand must already have a lot of the attributes associated with a cool brand – reputation, innovation, authenticity – and be inspirational and attractive, then employ a 'cool' PR agency to let the world know how great the brand is in an innovative/cool way.' **Jo Tutchener**

About the CoolBrands® book

August Media applies its refreshingly different approach to branded content, creating award-winning magazines, brochures and digital projects for some of the world's best-loved brands.

Founded in 2005 by some of consumer magazines' brightest stars, August Media is a feisty young agency whose success stems from a blend of professionalism, decades of experience, keen talent and a consuming passion for creative content. It's recognised as a different sort of agency from the mainstream because it thinks differently: more creatively, more astutely, more imaginatively. And it's this approach that made August the ideal choice for this year's CoolBrands® publication.

For CoolBrands® 2011/12, August Media's designers and editors worked closely with Superbrands to ensure that each brand is showcased in a clean, modern design that lets its unique identity shine through.

augustmedia.com

Qualifying CoolBrands® 2011/12

- 4 On Demand
- Abel & Cole
- Absolut
- Adidas
- Aesop
- Affordable Art Fair
- Aga
- Agent Provocateur
- Alain Ducasse at The Dorchester
- Alessi
- Alexander McQueen
- Alfa Romeo
- AllSaints
- Amazon.co.uk
- American Apparel
- American Express
- Anya Hindmarch
- Apple
- Aprilia
- Aquascutum
- Artisan du Chocolat
- Asahi
- Asos
- Aspall Cyder
- Aston Martin
- Atari
- Audi
- Aussie
- Aveda
- B&B Italia
- Babington House
- Bacardi
- Badoit
- Balenciaga
- BALTIC Centre for Contemporary Art
- Bang & Olufsen
- Barbican
- Barbour
- Barclaycard
- BBC
- BBC 1Xtra

- BBC 6 Music
- BBC iPlayer
- BBC Radio 1
- Beck's
- Belvedere Vodka
- Ben & Jerry's
- Benefit
- Bentley
- Berry Bros & Rudd
- Beyond Retro
- BFI Southbank
- Biba
- BlackBerry
- Blakes
- Blaupunkt
- BMW
- Bobbi Brown
- BoConcept
- Bodum
- Bollinger
- Bombay Sapphire
- Bose
- Bowers & Wilkins
- Brabantia
- Brian Atwood
- British Airways
- British Museum
- Browns
- Budweiser
- Budweiser Budvar
- Bulmers
- Bulthaup
- Bumble and Bumble
- Bungalow 8
- Burberry
- Burts Potato Chips
- Busaba Eathai
- Camilla Skovgaard
- Canon
- Cath Kidston
- Champagne Perrier-Jouët
- Chanel

- Channel 4
- Chantecaille
- Charbonnel et Walker
- Charles Heidsieck
- Chivas Regal
- Chloé
- Christian Louboutin
- Christopher Kane
- Cinnamon Kitchen
- Cirque du Soleil
- Clarins
- Clinique
- Cobra
- Coca-Cola
- Comme des Garçons
- Converse All Stars
- Corona Extra
- Corrigan's Mayfair
- COS
- Courvoisier
- Cowshed
- Crabbie's Alcoholic Ginger Beer
- Crème de la Mer
- Dave
- Daylesford Organic
- Dazed & Confused
- Decléor
- De'Longhi
- Dermalogica
- Design Hotels
- Design Museum
- Diesel
- Dior
- Diptyque
- Disaronno
- Divertimenti
- Dom Pérignon
- Dorset Cereals
- Dr. Hauschka
- Dr. Martens
- Dries Van Noten
- Ducati

- Dyson
- EA Games
- EA Sports
- EBay
- Eden Project
- Elemis
- Elite London
- Elle
- Elle Macpherson Intimates
- Emporio Armani
- Esquire
- Essie
- Estée Lauder
- Eurostar
- Eve Lom
- Evian
- Expedia
- Facebook
- Fairline
- Farrow & Ball
- Fentimans
- Ferrari
- Financial Times
- First Direct
- Flickr
- Fortnum & Mason
- Fred Perry
- Fresh! (Naturally Organic)
- Frieze Art Fair
- Fuji
- Gaggia
- Gap
- Georgina Goodman
- Ghd
- Givenchy
- Global Knives
- Globe-Trotter
- Godiva
- Google
- Gordon Ramsay
- Gordon's
- GQ

- Graham & Brown
- Graham & Green
- Grazia
- Green & Black's
- Grenson
- Grey Goose
- Grolsch
- Groupon
- Gü
- Gucci
- Guinness
- H&M
- Häagen-Dazs
- Habitat
- Hakkasan
- Hamleys
- Harley-Davidson
- Harper's Bazaar
- Harrods
- Harvey Nichols
- Haunch of Venison
- Havana Club
- Heal's
- Hendrick's
- Hennessy
- Hoegaarden
- Home House
- Hotel Chocolat
- Hotel du Vin
- HTC
- Hunter
- ICA
- I-D
- Ikea
- Illamasqua
- Illy
- Independent Talent
- Innocent
- Isabel Marant
- Issey Miyake
- Jack Daniel's
- Jägermeister
- Jaguar

- Jamie Oliver (Products)
- Jean Paul Gaultier
- Jelly Belly
- Jimmy Choo
- Jo Malone
- John Frieda
- John Lewis
- Johnnie Walker
- Jordans
- Jose Cuervo
- Kawasaki
- Kérastase
- Kettle Chips
- Kiehl's
- Kirin Ichiban
- Kiss
- KitchenAid
- Konami
- Krispy Kreme
- Kronenbourg 1664
- Krug
- Kurt Geiger
- La Maison du Chocolat
- La Perla
- La Prairie
- Lacoste
- Lamborghini
- Lancôme
- Land Rover
- Lara Bohinc
- L'Artisan Parfumeur
- Last.fm
- Lastminute.com
- L'Atelier de Joël Robuchon
- Laura Mercier
- Laurent-Perrier
- Lavazza
- Le Creuset
- Le Gavroche
- Le Labo
- Le Manoir aux Quat'Saisons

167

— Le Pain Quotidien
— Leffe
— Leica
— Leon
— Levi Roots
— Levi's
— Liberty
— Ligne Roset
— Lindt
— L'Occitane
— Lomography
— Lonely Planet
— Longchamp
— L'Oréal Paris
— Lotus
— Louis Roederer
— Lovefilm
— Lulu Guinness
— MAC
— Magners
— Maison Martin Margiela
— Malmaison
— Manolo Blahnik
— Marc Jacobs
— Marcus Wareing at The Berkeley
— Marks & Spencer
— Marmite
— Marni
— Marshall
— Martini
— Maserati
— MasterCard
— Matches
— Matthew Williamson
— Maybelline New York
— Mercedes-Benz
— Miele
— Mini
— Minx Nails
— Miu Miu
— Models 1
— Moët & Chandon

— Monocle
— Morgan
— Moschino
— Mr & Mrs Smith
— MTV
— Muji
— Mulberry
— Myla
— Namco
— Nars
— Neal's Yard Dairy
— Neal's Yard Remedies
— Neff
— Nespresso
— Net-A-Porter
— New Covent Garden Food Co.
— New York Bagel Company
— Nicholas Kirkwood
— Nike
— Nikon
— Nintendo
— Nobu London
— Nokia
— Nudie Jeans
— O2
— Oki-Ni
— Olympus
— Omega
— One Aldwych
— OPI Nails
— Orange
— Original Penguin
— Paperchase
— Patron Tequila
— Paul Smith
— Pentax
— Peroni Nastro Azzurro
— Perrier
— Piaggio
— Pimm's
— Piper-Heidsieck

— Planet Organic
— Play.com
— PlayStation
— Poggenpohl
— Porsche
— Power Plate
— Prada
— Pret A Manger
— Proud Galleries
— Puma
— Quintessentially
— Rachel's Organic
— Ralph Lauren
— Range Rover
— Ray-Ban
— Red Bull
— Reebok
— Reiss
— Rémy Martin
— Ren
— Rimmel London
— Roberts Radio
— Rococo Chocolates
— Rolex
— Rolls-Royce
— Rough Guides
— Rough Trade Shops
— Roundhouse
— Royal Albert Hall
— Royal Opera House
— Rubik's Cube
— Ruby & Millie
— Rude Health
— Russian Standard Vodka
— S.Pellegrino
— Saatchi Gallery
— Sailor Jerry
— Salty Dog
— Samsonite
— Samsung
— San Miguel
— Sanderson
— Sanderson (Hotel)

— Scalextric
— Sega
— Select Model Management
— Selfridges
— Sennheiser
— Shaun Leane
— Shazam
— Shiseido
— Shoreditch House
— Shortlist
— Shu Uemura
— Sky
— Skype
— Smeg
— Smirnoff
— Smythson of Bond Street
— Snog
— Sol
— Sony
— Sony Ericsson
— Southbank Centre
— Space.NK
— Spotify
— St John
— St Martins Lane
— St. Tropez
— Staropramen
— Stella Artois
— Stella McCartney
— Stephen Webster
— Stolichnaya
— Storm
— Streetcar
— Stylist
— Sunseeker
— Suzuki
— Swarovski
— Swatch
— Tag Heuer
— Taittinger

— Tanqueray gin
— Tate Modern
— Terry de Havilland
— The Cinnamon Club
— The Conran Shop
— The Daily Telegraph
— The Fat Duck
— The Groucho Club
— The Guardian
— The Hospital Club
— The Independent
— The May Fair
— The North Face
— The O2
— The Observer
— The Old Vic
— The Organic Pharmacy
— The River Café
— The Times
— The Wapping Project
— The White Company
— The Zetter
— Thierry Mugler
— Tiffany & Co.
— Tiger Beer
— Tigi
— Time Out Guides
— Tod's
— Tom Ford
— TomTom
— Top Trumps
— Topman
— Topshop
— Trailfinders
— Triumph
— Tropicana
— TsingTao
— Tweezerman
— Twinings
— Twitter
— TŶ Nant
— Uniqlo
— Urban Junkies

— Urban Outfitters
— V&A
— Vaio
— Vanessa Bruno
— Vans
— Vespa
— Veuve Clicquot
— ViewLondon.co.uk
— Villeroy & Boch
— Virgin Atlantic
— Virgin Media
— Visa
— Vitra
— Vivienne Westwood
— Vodafone
— Vogue
— VV Rouleaux
— W Hotel
— Wagamama
— WAH Nails
— Wahaca
— Waitrose
— Wallpaper*
— Wallpaper* City Guides
— Westfield
— Whistles
— Whole Foods Market
— Wolford
— Wonderbra
— Xbox
— XFM
— Yauatcha
— Yeo Valley
— YMC
— YouTube
— YSL
— Zara
— Zubrowka